Famous Friends:

Maya Angelou
AND
Oprah Winfrey

*How They Met, Their Humble Beginnings
and Amazing Achievements*

Tamra B. Orr

CURIOUS
FOX
BOOKS

ABOUT THE AUTHOR: Tamra B. Orr is a full-time author living in the Pacific Northwest with her family. She graduated from Ball State University in Muncie, Indiana. She has written more than 500 books about everything from historical events and career choices to controversial issues and celebrity biographies. On those rare occasions that she is not writing a book, she is reading one.

© 2024 by Curious Fox Books™, an imprint of Fox Chapel Publishing Company, Inc., 903 Square Street, Mount Joy, PA 17552.

Famous Friends: Maya Angelou and Oprah Winfrey is a revision of *Famous Friends: True Tales of Friendship: Maya Angelou and Oprah Winfrey*, published in 2020 by Purple Toad Publishing, Inc. Reproduction of its contents is strictly prohibited without written permission from the rights holder.

PUBLISHER'S NOTE: This story has not been authorized by Oprah Winfrey or the estate of Maya Angelou.

Paperback ISBN 979-8-89094-016-2
Hardcover ISBN 979-8-89094-017-9

Library of Congress Control Number: 2023952476

To learn more about the other great books from Fox Chapel Publishing, or to find a retailer near you, call toll-free 800-457-9112 or visit us at *www.FoxChapelPublishing.com*.

We are always looking for talented authors. To submit an idea, please send a brief inquiry to acquisitions@foxchapelpublishing.com.

Fox Chapel Publishing makes every effort to use environmentally friendly paper for printing.

Printed in China

CONTENTS

The caged bird was an important symbol to author Maya Angelou (top), and one that spoke to Oprah Winfrey's heart.

"Meeting Myself"

Have you ever picked up a book and felt like the author was speaking right to you? Perhaps a character behaves exactly the way you would in a similar situation. Maybe he or she has thoughts or ideas that exactly mirror your own. It is a wonderful feeling—like you have found someone who truly understands you and what you are going through.

That is exactly what happened when a teenager named Oprah Winfrey picked up a copy of *I Know Why the Caged Bird Sings*, a book by author and poet Maya Angelou. She read the words and, for the first time in her life, felt like she was understood. "I read it over and over," Winfrey wrote in an essay. "I had never before read a book that validated my own existence."[1] The two women had struggled with some of the same problems, including loneliness and trauma. The fact that Angelou had overcome these issues and grown into a successful poet and author helped Winfrey realize that she could, too. Years later, in her magazine, *O*, Winfrey recalled, "With each page, [Angelou's] life seemed to mirror mine. . . . Meeting Maya on those pages was like meeting myself in full. For the first time, as a young black girl, my experience was validated."[2] It was a true turning point for her.

The young Winfrey did not know it at the time, but the author she so connected with would end up becoming not only her mentor and inspiration, but also one of her closest personal friends. The two women first met in the 1970s when the young Winfrey was a television reporter in Baltimore, Maryland. While working at WJZ-TV in Baltimore as a TV reporter, she was given the chance to interview many different people, and one day that included her role model, Maya Angelou. "When I was 22 or 23 years old, I had the great fortune of interviewing her [Angelou]," Winfrey told reporter Roland Martin in 2014. "I said to her, 'If you would just give me five minutes of your time, Miss Angelou.' At the end of those

Little did Winfrey know that one day she would be as famous as her favorite writer.

With the help of Angelou's writing, Winfrey was able to overcome painful experiences from her childhood.

five minutes, she said to me, 'Who are you girl?' And we have been friends ever since."[3]

Over the years, Winfrey and Angelou became each other's friends, advisers, and teachers. Winfrey interviewed Angelou a number of times

The Mayan ruins stretch out across southern Mexico, Gutatemala, Honduras, and Belize. The ruins were one of the stops on the birthday cruise.

on both her daily talk show, *Oprah*, and in her publication, *O, The Oprah Magazine*. In addition, the two women spent time together.

On the author's 70th birthday in April 1998, Winfrey hosted a huge party for her. More than one hundred of Angelou's friends sailed on a cruise ship to the Mayan ruins in Mexico.

It was a grand event. As Winfrey stated in her magazine, "Since I can remember, having fun for me always has involved sharing what I had or was doing with someone else. When Maya Angelou turned 70, I wanted to celebrate and honor her life in a big way, have some major good fun." It

The *Seabourn Pride* carried Winfrey and many other friends of Angelou's to exotic destinations.

took more than a year to plan the party. "It was a wild week," Winfrey continued, "made even more fun because most of the people there had known Maya her entire life. And for the guests—educators, authors, businesspeople, artists—this was a chance to let go of everyday restraints and responsibilities and just play. It was the most fun I've ever had, watching so many other people have a blast."[4]

From the moment a teenage Winfrey opened Angelou's book for the first time, until the day Angelou died in 2014 and Winfrey tearfully spoke at her funeral, the two women were a beacon of what friendship can be. They inspired each other, supported each other, amused each other—and learned from each other. Theirs is what friendship is all about.

Oprah Winfrey interviewed more than 30,000 people on *The Oprah Winfrey Show* from 1986 to 2011, including numerous interviews with Maya Angelou. One of her interviews with Maya was on the last episode of the show in 2011.

Maya Angelou wrote stories and poetry that spoke to the hearts of many people, including Oprah Winfrey.

I Know Why THe Caged Bird Sing

I Know Why the Caged Bird Sings was the first book by an African American woman to become a nonfiction bestseller. It inspired many other black writers to tell their own stories. The autobiography was made into a movie in 1979, and Angelou cowrote the screenplay. The book became a bestseller again in 1993 after Angelou read one of her poems at Bill Clinton's presidential inauguration.

In 2009, a special anniversary edition of the book was issued. The publisher asked Oprah to write the foreword to it. She wrote, "Maya Angelou lived what she wrote. She understood that sharing her truth connected her to the greater human truths—of longing, abandonment, security, hope, wonder, prejudice, mystery, and finally self-discovery: the realization of who you really are and the liberation that love brings. And each of those timeless truths unfolds in this first autobiographical account of her life."[5]

Angelou was a very popular speaker at all kinds of events because of the passion and truth in her words.

As a preschooler, Winfrey performed in Old Buffalo Church in Kosciusko, Mississippi. People had a hard time pronouncing her given name, Orpah. (Orpah is a name from the Bible.) They called her Oprah instead.

Overcoming Obstacles

When teenage Oprah Winfrey first read Maya Angelou's words, she was in great need of the hope she found there. She was born on January 29, 1954, in Kosciusko, Mississippi, to young parents, Vernita Lee and Vernon Winfrey. They were not married, and shortly after the girl's birth, they split up completely. Oprah, whose birth name was Orpah Gail, was largely raised by her grandmother, Hattie Mae Lee. Hattie was a strong believer in doing chores, going to church, and physically disciplining children.

It was clear from a very early age that Oprah was smart. She was reading by the age of three, and skipped several grades in elementary school. Although she did well in school, she struggled with her family, often splitting her time among her mother's and father's separate homes and her grandmother's. She was left alone too often, or worse, under the care of an abusive teenage cousin.

Turning It Around
By 1968, Winfrey was stealing money, skipping school, and running away. At age 14, she found herself pregnant. When the baby died a few weeks

While Oprah attended East National High School, her life changed in many ways—leading her in new and better directions.

after he was born, Winfrey felt like life could not get any worse. Then her father gave her no choice but to focus on school and her education, and her life changed. It changed even more when she read Maya Angelou's autobiography and realized that she was not as alone as she thought she was. Like her, Angelou had dealt with abuse and feeling unloved and unwanted. "When you see other people who have come through the worst, survived what you're going through, that lets you know you can," she said in the documentary *MAKERS: Women Who Make America*.[1]

Winfrey concentrated on school and soon graduated high school with honors. Her hard work earned her a scholarship to Tennessee State University (TSU). After leaving TSU, she worked for WTVF-TV in Nashville. A few years later, she moved to Baltimore to work as a TV news anchor for WJZ-TV and soon was given her own talk show *People Are Talking*. This opportunity working for WJZ-TV was where Winfrey would interview Angelou for the first time and was only the beginning of what would become a stellar career.

A Household Name

Ever since Winfrey had recited Bible verses in church as a child and won a speech contest in high school, she realized she not only enjoyed talking to people, but she was good at it. By 1986, she had her own national daily talk show, interviewing everyone from heroes and celebrities to everyday people with important stories to share. *The Oprah Winfrey Show* ran for a total of 25 seasons—almost 5,000 episodes. It had millions of viewers every afternoon. The show was broadcast in more than 100 countries around the

Oprah started her own television studio. She used her name spelled backwards as its title.

world and, over the years, it earned 48 awards. Even though Oprah became one of the most popular talk-show hosts of all time, she returned to TSU and graduated in 1986. That same year, she also met her life partner Stedman Graham.

Winfrey expanded far beyond her talk show, however. She appeared in a variety of movies and television series. She founded her own television company (Harpo Studios) and a cable station—OWN—with programming for women. She started a magazine, plus wrote seven books. She created Oprah's Book Club, the largest reading group ever known, with more than two million members.

The Oprah Winfrey Leadership Academy for Girls opened in 2007 and has continued today for more than a decade.

By 2019, Winfrey was considered one of the most generous philanthropists in the world, donating millions and millions of dollars to many charities and organizations. She founded the Leadership Academy for Girls near Johannesburg, South Africa. The Oprah Winfrey Association has provided food, clothing, shoes, books, and school supplies to more than 50,000 children. She has created scholarships, helped women's shelters, and created youth centers. She has done all of these things because, as she explained in a speech at the Forbes 400 Summit on Philanthropy, she realized "the only way to create long-term improvement and empowerment, and literally change the trajectory of somebody's life, is through education."[2]

An Award Winner

Winfrey has won almost every possible award for her hard work and her dedication to helping others. In 2013, President Barack Obama gave her the nation's highest award a civilian can earn: the Presidential Medal of Freedom. Although Winfrey is often listed as one of the most successful, wealthy, and generous women in the world, she still remembers being lost, alone, and scared. When she received the Cecil B. DeMille lifetime achievement award in 2018, she took a moment to speak directly to all of those young people who might find themselves in need of support. Referencing the #MeToo Movement, which is dedicated to stopping sexual abuse, she said:

Receiving the Presidential Medal of Freedom from President Obama was one of the Oprah's proudest moments.

In my career, what I've always tried my best to do, whether on television or through film, is to say something about how men and women really behave: to say how we experience shame, how we love and how we rage, how we fail, how we retreat, persevere, and how we overcome. And I've interviewed and portrayed people who've withstood some of the ugliest things life can throw at you, but the one quality all of them seem to share is an ability to maintain hope for a brighter morning—even during our darkest nights."[3]

Oprah has inspired and motivated countless people to change their lives for the better.

The courage and determination Winfrey shows the world every day is, in large part, thanks to her friendship with Maya Angelou. As she has stated in many interviews, no other person in her life has had more influence on her.

Becoming Mrs. Which

In 2018, Oprah Winfrey played the part of Mrs. Which in the Disney film *A Wrinkle in Time*. Her role as a supernova, or celestial being, was bigger than life—literally—and complete with mystery and magic. Not too surprisingly, the way she played Mrs. Which was largely based on her friend Maya Angelou. "For me, she was a cross between Maya Angelou, who was a mentor, friend, mother figure for me, and Glinda the Good Witch, who is my favorite all-time mythical magical character," she explained to *People* magazine. "You have a little bit of Glinda, and then you have a lot of Maya," she added. "And so you combine the two and put me in the center as the vessel for it and you get Mrs. Which." Winfrey loved the role, citing it as one of the best experiences of her career. "Honestly, to be playing a supernova, who uses her wisdom to help guide these children in their path to what's right and good toward the light, I mean—hello, speaking my language in every way."[4]

Oprah shares the stage with her co-stars from *A Wrinkle in Time*, including Chris Pine and Reese Witherspoon (center).

Maya Angelou's first home (top) was in St. Louis. By the time she was 42 (left), she had traveled the world and published her first bestseller.

Train Conductor to Civil Rights Activist

Marguerite Annie Johnson knew what it was like to struggle. The girl who would be known as Maya Angelou was born in April 1928 in St. Louis, Missouri. Her parents, Bailey Johnson and Vivian Baxter, split up when she was young, so she and her brother Bailey Jr. were sent to live with their grandmother in Arkansas. One day, when visiting her mother, Marguerite Angelou was attacked. When she told her brother what had happened, he told relatives. Her attacker was sent to jail and was killed after he was released.

The young girl was so overwhelmed by what her words had done, she stopped speaking to anyone but her brother—for almost five years. "I decided that my voice was so powerful that it could kill people, but it could not harm my brother because we loved each other so much," she later wrote in *The Guardian*. "My mother and her family tried to woo me away from mutism, but they didn't know what I knew: that my voice was a killing machine."[1]

When Marguerite became a teenager, her life changed. She went to San Francisco to live with her mother, and began talking once again. She won a scholarship to study dance and drama at San Francisco's Labor School. She dropped out within a year, but her love of dance remained.

At 16, Marguerite decided she wanted to be a streetcar conductor. She had seen women riding on the streetcars in San Francisco and liked how they looked. "They had caps with bills on them and form-fitting jackets," she told her friend Oprah Winfrey in an interview in May 2013. "I loved the uniforms, so I said 'That's the job I want!'" The streetcar company had never hired a black person before, let alone a 16-year-old female. When she first asked for an application, the company refused to give her one. When she told her mother, Baxter told her to go back and sit in the office every single day and "read one of your big thick Russian books." She then advised her to remain there until the end of the day when everyone left. While waiting, she was teased and insulted, but she stayed. "I sat there because I was afraid to go home," she told Oprah. "I was afraid to tell my mother that I was not as strong as she thought I was."[2]

Marguerite sat in that office every day for two weeks. Finally, the cable car company gave her the job. Every morning, Angelou got up at 4 a.m., put on the uniform she so loved, and went to work. To make sure she stayed safe while riding the streetcar, her mother followed the route in her car. Later, Baxter told her daughter that she had learned a

"I've learned that people will forget what you said, people will forget what you did, but people will never forget how you made them feel." —Maya Angelou

Streetcars were like trains, but their tracks ran along city streets. They were common in most large US cities from about the 1890s until the 1960s.

great deal about herself from the job. "You learned that you are very strong and that with determination and dedication you can go anywhere in the world."[3]

From the Stage to Civil Rights

In 1945, Marguerite had a new experience: she became a mother. She named her son Clyde Bailey "Guy" Johnson. To take care of her new baby, she held a variety of jobs, from nightclub dancer to Creole café cook. "The birth of my son caused me to develop the courage to invent my life," she stated in the book *Carpe Diem Regained*.[4]

By the 1950s, Johnson was acting, singing, and dancing in theater plays and television variety shows. In 1949, she briefly married a Greek sailor, Anastasios Angelopulos. She would use a form of his last name, Angelou, from then on.

Dr. Martin Luther King, Jr., and his wife, Coretta, were two of the primary leaders of the US civil rights movement.

In 1957, Angelou recorded a music album, *Miss Calypso*. As the decade ended, she settled in New York and got involved with the city's active civil rights movement. She temporarily lived in Cairo, Egypt, where she met South African civil rights activist Vusumzi Make. Some historians have stated the two soon married, while others state that they were in a relationship and lived together. After they split up, she and her son moved to Ghana in 1962. When her son was in a terrible car accident and his neck was broken, she focused on helping him heal and eventually recover. While in Cairo and Ghana, Angelou began writing and editing articles for local newspapers. She learned how to speak French, Spanish, Italian, Arabic, and Fanti (a language spoken in West Africa). She also met and began working with minister and civil rights leader Malcolm X in Ghana.

In 1964, Angelou and Guy returned to the United States. Soon after, she began working for civil rights with Dr. Martin Luther King, Jr. She was so devastated when he was assassinated on her birthday in 1968 that for many years she quit celebrating her birthday. Instead, she would send flowers to King's widow, Coretta Scott King.

Over the years, many people encouraged Angelou to write about some of her life experiences. In *I Know Why the Caged Bird Sings*, she wrote of her childhood until the age of 16. The book was published in 1969 and was a huge success.

Angelou's star was on the rise. She was named to the National Commission on the Observance of International Women's Year by President Jimmy Carter. This group helps organize International Women's Day events with similar

The International Women's Day March draws thousands of people every year.

organizations around the world. Women's Day is celebrated on March 8 and focuses on promoting global civil rights for women.

Soon, Angelou became the first African American female director in Hollywood. She acted in and directed several movies, including *All Day Long*, *Look Away*, and *Roots*. Meanwhile, she married Paul Du Feu in 1973; they divorced eight years later.

Sharing her Stories

I Know Why the Caged Bird Sings was Angelou's first autobiography, but not her last. She wrote additional autobiographies, as well as books of poetry, including *Gather Together in My Name*, *Singin' and Swingin' and Gettin' Merry Like*, *The Heart of a Woman*, *All God's Children Need Traveling Shoes* and *A Song Flung Up to Heaven*. She was in high demand as a teacher and a speaker throughout the world.

When president-elect Bill Clinton asked Angelou to read her poem "On the Pulse of the Morning" at his inauguration in 1993, it was a wonderful moment for the poet and writer. In part, the poem read,

Here on the pulse of this new day
You may have the grace to look up and out
And into your sister's eyes, into
Your brother's face, your country
And say simply
Very simply
With hope
Good morning.[5]

Her reading of the poem was broadcast live around the world.

In 1998, Angelou became an official movie director with her film *Down in the Delta*. Two years later, she was given the Presidential Medal of the Arts, and in 2011, President Barack Obama awarded her the Presidential Medal of

When Angelou read part of her poem at Bill Clinton's inauguration, it was many people's introduction to the author.

Freedom—two years before Winfrey was given the same medal. It was just another one of many things these two women had in common.

Becoming "Maya Angelou"

How did Marguerite Annie Johnson become Maya Angelou? As a child, her brother Bailey was unable to say her name, so he called her My for "my sister." Later, after reading a book about the Mayan Native Americans, he began calling her Maya. She liked the name and kept it. Her last name came from a brief marriage in 1949 to Anastasios Angelopulos. She began using the name when dancing or appearing on stage. Over time, the name stuck, and Maya Angelou became Marguerite's permanent new name.

Marguerite became Maya, another way that she moved beyond her past and created a better future.

In 2012, First Lady Michelle Obama (left) and celebrity Queen Latifah presented Angelou with the Literary Arts Award at the BET Honors ceremony.

CHAPTER 4

Kindred Spirits

It is easy to see why Oprah Winfrey and Maya Angelou became such good friends. They shared many of the same childhood experiences, from parents who separated early to strict grandmothers, assault to early pregnancies. They also shared the determination and courage to overcome those issues and become strong, powerful women.

The first time Winfrey went to Angelou's home, she was still an awestruck fan. "She was the biggest rock star in the world to me, and now I'm sitting in her house," she told *International Business Times*.[1] During the visit, Angelou cooked for her new friend, and then read poetry by Paul Laurence Dunbar (the first nationally recognized African American poet) aloud to Winfrey. While Winfrey was there, Angelou gave her some advice that still guides Winfrey's life. After discussing many of the mistakes Winfrey felt she had made in her life so far, Angelou said, "That was in your 20s, and now you're in your 30s. When you know better, you do better."[2] Winfrey loved that expression so much that she used it repeatedly on her daily television show. "Not only did I share, every chance I got to say those words, I did," she said in an interview in 2016. "Exactly 43

In 2016, Winfrey appeared with US Ambassador Patrick Gaspard in South Africa to speak about how women can overcome challenges.

times!" she added. "Do you know how freeing those words are? How freeing they can be for you? What they mean is that you don't have to hold yourself hostage to who you used to be or anything you ever used to do. Because who has lived and hasn't made mistakes?"[3]

Sharing Time, Food, and Advice

Over the years, Angelou acted as both friend and mentor to Winfrey, often sharing important advice to the younger woman. "She's the woman who

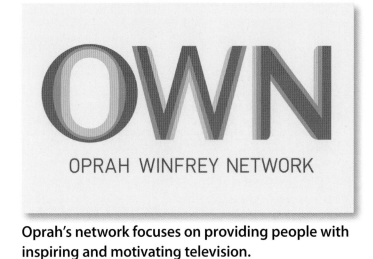

Oprah's network focuses on providing people with inspiring and motivating television.

can share my triumphs, chide me with hard truth and soothe me with words of comfort when I call her in my deepest pain," she wrote in her magazine.[4] Angelou appeared on *The Oprah Winfrey Show* in 2004 and 2011, as well as on two episodes of OWN's *Super Soul Sunday* in 2013.

Winfrey went to Angelou's house often, and it became like a second home to her. "It is here, in Maya's home, that I feel as comfortable as I do in my own," she wrote in her magazine. "At the table where we always flop down and catch up, in the sculpture garden in her backyard, in the kitchen where the sweet smell of pumpkin soup wafts through the air. When I am with Maya, unimportant matters melt away—her presence feels like a warm bath after an exhausting day. In our hours together, we can set aside all pretensions and just be: two women barefoot in a living room, sharing the most intimate parts of our lives."[5] The two women conducted one of their favorite interviews together in

Maya Angelou had wit and wisdom to spare when chatting with people.

Oprah and Maya had more than their friendship in common. They also focused on taking their life lessons and sharing them with others.

1997 sitting on a big brass bed in pajamas, having a televised "slumber party" while they discussed Angelou's new book, *The Heart of a Woman*.

For many years, the two women—so close in experience and spirit—remained friends. They shared heartaches, celebrations, and insight into living a better life. It was a friendship that made both of their lives better—the best kind of connection.

Negative and Positive Power

In one of Winfrey's multiple interviews with Angelou, they discussed the power of negative and positive statements in life. "I believe that a negative statement is poison," Angelou explained to her friend. "I'm convinced that the negative has power. It lives. And if you allow it to perch in your house, in your mind, in your life, it can take you over. So when the rude or cruel thing is said, . . . I say, 'Take it all out of my house!' Those negative words climb into the woodwork and into the furniture, and the next thing you know they'll be on my skin." And what about the positive power? "You can ask it in, show it how much you like it, make room for it," Angelou said. "And it says, 'Oh, I like this place, I think I'll stay here.'"[6]

In 2008, at the age of 80, Angelou still spoke to audiences and shared her love of life.

Angelou considered herself a teacher first, writer second. She taught at Wake Forest University in North Carolina for many years, earning an honorary degree in 1977.

A Lifelong Friendship

By 2014, Maya Angelou, now 86 years old, was slowing down. She had trouble seeing clearly and spent much of her time in a wheelchair. In early April, just after her birthday, the National Portrait Gallery unveiled a large painting of her that would later be hung in the Smithsonian Institution. The gallery's mission was to display the individuals who have helped to shape American culture. Artist Ross Rossin created the photo-like painting from a variety of historical and current photos of the writer. "I have a portrait of my grandmother in my home," Angelou said. "It's an honor for African Americans, of course. Then it is an honor for Jews and Arabs, Irish and Italians—all the people who came to America hoping to leave a portrait of themselves for those who are left to come, those who came looking for freedom."[1]

On May 28, 2014, Angelou died unexpectedly—and the world mourned. People around the world, including several former presidents, reached out to send their thoughts to the family. Barack Obama said, "Over the course

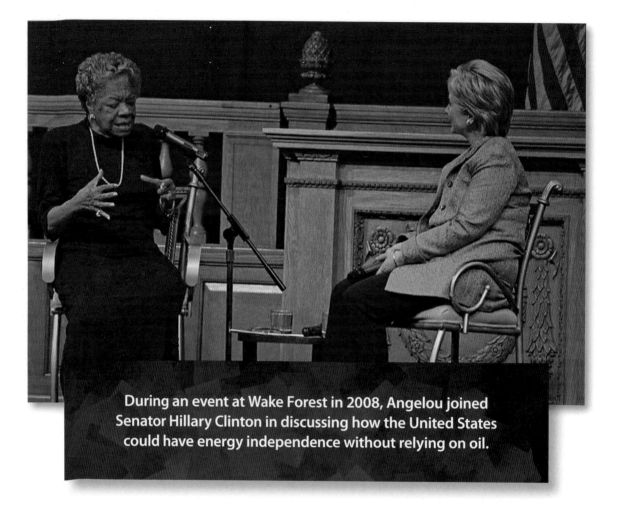

During an event at Wake Forest in 2008, Angelou joined Senator Hillary Clinton in discussing how the United States could have energy independence without relying on oil.

of her remarkable life, Maya was many things—an author, poet, civil rights activist, playwright, actress, director, composer, singer and dancer. But above all, she was a storyteller—and her greatest stories were true. A childhood of suffering and abuse actually drove her to stop speaking—but the voice she found helped generations of Americans find their rainbow amidst the clouds, and inspired the rest of us to be our best selves. In fact, she inspired my own mother to name my sister Maya."[2]

Bill Clinton stated, "The poems and stories she wrote and read to us in her commanding voice were gifts of wisdom and wit, courage and grace. I will always be grateful for her electrifying reading of 'On the Pulse of Morning' at my first inaugural, and even more for all the years of friendship that followed."[3] In addition, George W. Bush said, "Her words inspired peace and equality and enriched the culture of our country. We are grateful for the work she leaves behind, and we wish her the peace she always sought."[4]

In 1993, Maya Angelou (second from right), along with other important women from the Black Women's Leadership Group, met with President Bill Clinton in the White House.

Of course, one of the people most impacted by the loss of Maya Angelou was Oprah Winfrey. She posted the following message on her website:

> I've been blessed to have Maya Angelou as my mentor, mother/sister and friend since my 20s. She was there for me always, guiding me through some of the most important years of my life. The world knows her as a poet, but at the heart of her, she was a teacher. 'When you learn, teach. When you get, give' is one of my best lessons from her. . . But what stands out to me most about Maya Angelou is not what she has done or written or spoken; it's how she lived her life. She moved through the world with unshakable calm, confidence and a fierce grace. I loved her, and I know she loved me. I will profoundly miss her. She will always be the rainbow in my clouds."[5]

Since she lost her dear friend, Winfrey has worked to honor her. In March 2015, she, along with Postmaster General Megan Brennan, announced the new Maya Angelou Forever stamp. The stamp features Rossin's image of the poet and features a quote by author Joan Walsh Augland that links to Angelou's first book: "A bird doesn't sing because it has an answer, it sings because it has a song."[6]

In 2018, the National Museum of African American History and Culture dedicated a 4,300-square-foot exhibition

"I'm convinced of this: Good done anywhere is good done everywhere. For a change, start by speaking to people rather than walking by them like they're stones that don't matter. As long as you're breathing, it's never too late to do some good." Maya Angelou

Artist Kate Merriman's tribute to Maya Angelou

to the life and accomplishments of Oprah Winfrey. It includes more than 200 artifacts—from one of her interview couches from her daily show to a costume she wore in one of her movies. Museum director Lonnie Bunch III stated, "Just as Oprah Winfrey watched TV coverage of the civil rights movement and was shaped by the era in which she was born and raised, she has gone on to have a profound effect on how Americans view themselves and each other in the tumultuous decades that followed. She

Years of African-American history are on display at the National Museum of African American History. Visitors can find Harriet Tubman's hymnal and even the Bible of Nat Turner. They can also find items from Winfrey's iconic talk show.

has a place in the museum with a long line of women who did extraordinary things in their time—Harriet Tubman, Sojourner Truth, Ida B. Wells, Maya Angelou—women who worked to redeem the soul of America."[7]

There is no doubt that Winfrey and Angelou were two quite extraordinary women—and they had an extraordinary friendship.

At Angelou's memorial, former First Lady Michelle Obama honored the amazing woman and her achievements.

And Still I Rise

In 2017, the two-hour documentary *Maya Angelou: And Still I Rise* premiered on PBS as part of the station's American Masters series. It features excerpts from some of Angelou's best interviews, and it includes moments with Angelou's friends, colleagues, and family for deeper insight into her life. Director Rita Coburn Whack admitted, "Pulling it all together was a challenge. I wanted more than anything for people to see her as a whole person—her frailties, her strengths—so that you knew that this is something you could do. . . . She was not trying to be Maya Angelou, she was trying to survive. It was important to humanize her. . . . You're not just defined by being nominated for the National Book Award or getting a Grammy, but you're also defined by what hurts and hits us."

Bob Hercules, the film's co-director, added, "What I always wondered was how she accomplished all these things. I realized that she had for whatever reason instilled in her—maybe by her grandmother, maybe by having to go through the trials of racism, the trial of the rape—she had amazing courage: The courage to take on things that others wouldn't."[8]

In that way, she inspired not only Oprah Winfrey, but people around the world.

In 2011, Maya received a presidential medal—an honor few people achieve in their lifetimes.

1928	Marguerite Annie "Maya" Johnson is born in St. Louis, Missouri on April 4.
1944	Maya gets a job as a streetcar conductor.
1945	Her son, Clyde Bailey "Guy" Johnson is born.
1949	Maya briefly marries Anastasios Angelopulos. She begins using the stage name Maya Angelou, and eventually fully adopts the name.
1954	Orpah Gail Winfrey is born in Kosciusko, Mississippi, on January 29.
1957	Angelou releases the album *Miss Calypso*.
1964	Angelou begins working with civil rights activist Dr. Martin Luther King, Jr.
1968	Winfrey runs away. She gets pregnant, but the baby comes too early and dies.
1969	*I Know Why the Caged Bird Sings* is published and becomes a bestseller.
1971	Winfrey enrolls in Tennessee State University to study communication and performing arts.
1974	Winfrey meets Angelou when she interviews her in Baltimore. The women become fast friends.
1979	*I Know Why the Caged Bird Sings* is made into a movie.
1984	Winfrey moves to Chicago to host *The Oprah Winfrey Show*.
1986	*The Oprah Winfrey Show* begins to air daily. Oprah returned to Tennessee State University to complete her degree and graduated. She founds Harpo Productions.
1988	The International Television and Radio Society names Winfrey Broadcaster of the Year.
1993	Angelou recites a poem at the Clinton inauguration. *I Know Why the Caged Bird Sings* becomes a bestseller again.
1996	Winfrey launches Oprah's Book Club.
1998	Winfrey hosts a cruise for Angelou's 70th birthday; Angelou directs her first film.
2000	Winfrey launches *O, The Oprah Magazine*. Angelou is awarded the Presidential Medal of the Arts.
2007	Winfrey creates the Leadership Academy for Girls.
2009	Winfrey writes the foreword to a special anniversary edition of *I Know Why the Caged Bird Sings*.
2011	President Barack Obama awards Angelou the Presidential Medal of Freedom.
2013	President Obama awards Winfrey the Presidential Medal of Freedom.
2014	Angelou's portrait is added to the Smithsonian National Portrait Gallery. She dies at age 86.
2015	Angelou's portrait is used to make a Forever postage stamp.
2017	The documentary *Maya Angelou: And Still I Rise* is released on PBS.
2018	Winfrey receives the Cecil B. DeMille Award for lifetime achievement; she is given a display at the National Museum of African American History and Culture.

Chapter One. "Meeting Myself"

1. Salley, Columbus. *The Black 100: A Ranking of the Most Influential African-Americans, Past and Present* (New York: Citadel Press, 1999), p. 326.
2. Winfrey, Oprah. "Oprah Talks to Maya Angelou." *O, the Oprah Magazine*, December 2000.
3. Martin, Roland. "Roland Martin Interviews Oprah about Her Relationship with Maya Angelou." YouTube, April 12, 2014.
4. Winfrey, Oprah. "The Most Fun I Ever Had." *O, the Oprah Magazine*, May 2002. h
5. Afrobella. "In Case You Need a New Copy of *I Know Why the Caged Bird Sings*." *Afrobella*, March 26, 2015.

Chapter Two: Overcoming Obstacles

1. "All about Oprah: Winfrey Reflects on Her Life History in 'MAKERS Documentary.' " *HuffPost*, February 28, 2013.
2. Forbes, Moira. "Oprah Winfrey Talks Philanthropy, Failure and What Every Guest—Including Beyonce—Asks Her." *Forbes*, September 18, 2012.
3. Winfrey, Oprah. "Oprah Winfrey's Golden Globes Cecil B DeMille Speech—In Full." *The Telegraph*. January 8, 2018.
4. Miller, Mike. "Oprah Winfrey on How Her 'Mother Figure' Maya Angelou Inspired Her *A Wrinkle in Time* Character." *People*, May 29, 2018.

Chapter Three: Train Conductor to Civil Rights Activist

1. Angelou, Maya. "Maya Angelou: My Terrible, Wonderful Mother." *The Guardian*, March 30, 2013.
2. Oprah.com. "How Dr. Maya Angelou Became San Francisco's First Black Streetcar Conductor." *Super Soul Sunday*, Season 4, Episode 410, May 12, 2013.
3. Ibid.
4. Krznarik, Roman. *Carpe Diem Regained*. New York: Penguin Random House, 2017.
5. Angelou, Maya. "On the Pulse of Morning."

Chapter Four. Kindred Spirits

1. Killoran, Ellen. "For Oprah Winfrey, Maya Angelou's Death Especially Personal." *International Business Times*, May 28, 2014.
2. Bertram, Colin. "Oprah Winfrey Remembers Her 'Mentor' Maya Angelou." NBC Washington, May 28, 2014.
3. "Oprah Winfrey Mourns Maya Angelou." UPI. *U.S. News*, May 29, 2014.
4. Winfrey, Oprah. "Oprah Talks to Maya Angelou." *O, The Oprah Magazine*, December 2000.
5. Ibid.
6. Ibid.

Chapter Five. A Lifelong Friendship

1. Thompson, Krissah. "Honored by National Portrait Gallery, Maya Angelou Faces Mortality and Immortality." *The Washington Post*, April 6, 2014.
2. WEB Staff, "Oprah Posts Loving Tribute to Maya Angelou." CBS Channel 6, May 28, 2014.
3. Ibid.
4. Ibid.
5. Oldenburg, Ann. "Oprah Remembers Maya Angelou as 'Mentor, Mother/Sister, and Friend.'" *USA Today*, May 28, 2014.
6. Dwyer, Colin. "USPS Picks Perfect Line for Maya Angelou Stamp—If Only It Were Hers." NPR, April 8, 2015.
7. Cascone, Sarah. "She's Not President (Yet), But Oprah Winfrey Has Already Taken Over DC—as an Art Exhibition." *ArtNet News*, June 8, 2018.
8. Walk-Morris, Tatiana. "Oprah and the Clintons Celebrate Maya Angelou in a New Documentary." *Vice*, February 21, 2017.

Books

Creager, Ellen. *Oprah Winfrey (Women Who Won't Be Silenced: The Stories of Strong Women)*. San Diego: Lucent Books, 2019.

Keppeler, Jill. *Maya Angelou (Heroes of Black History)*. New York: Gareth Stevens, 2019.

Kramer, Barbara. *Who Is Oprah Winfrey?* New York: Penguin Workshop, 2019.

Labrecque, Ellen. *Who Was Maya Angelou?* New York: Penguin Workshop, 2016.

Medina, Melissa, and Fredrik Colting. *What I Can Learn from the Incredible and Fantastic Life of Oprah Winfrey*. Los Angeles: Moppet Books, 2017.

Nelson, Kristen R. *Maya Angelou: African American Poet*. New York: Enslow Publishers, 2019.

Orr, Tamra. *Oprah Winfrey*. Kennett Square, PA: Purple Toad Publishing, 2018.

On the Internet

Biography of Maya Angelou and of Oprah Winfrey from Ducksters at https://www.ducksters.com/biography/authors/mayaangelou.php and https://www.ducksters.com/biography/entertainers/oprah_winfrey.php

Trivia and a video about Maya Angelou and about Oprah Winfrey from Fun Facts at http://www.fun-facts.org.uk/black-americans/maya-angelou.htm and http://www.fun-facts.org.uk/black-americans/oprah-winfrey.htm

Works Consulted

Afrobella. "In Case You Need a New Copy of *I Know Why the Caged Bird Sings*." *Afrobella*, March 26, 2015. https://www.afrobella.com/2015/03/26/i-know-why-the-caged-bird-sings-oprah-foreword/

"All about Oprah: Winfrey Reflects on Her Life History in 'MAKERS Documentary.'" *HuffPost*, February 28, 2013. https://www.huffingtonpost.com/2013/02/28/about-oprah-winfrey-life-history-makers_n_2760337.html

Angelou, Maya. "Maya Angelou: My Terrible, Wonderful Mother." *The Guardian*, Marcy 30, 2013. https://www.theguardian.com/books/2013/mar/30/maya-angelou-terrible-wonderful-mother

Angelou, Maya. "On the Pulse of Morning." https://genius.com/Maya-angelou-on-the-pulse-of-morning-annotated

Bertram, Colin. "Oprah Winfrey Remembers Her 'Mentor' Maya Angelou." NBC Washington, May 28, 2014. https://www.nbcnewyork.com/news/national-international/oprah-winfrey-remembers-maya-angelou-mentor-mother-sister-friend/1002894/

Cascone, Sarah. "She's Not President (Yet), But Oprah Winfrey Has Already Taken Over DC—As an Art Exhibition." *ArtNet News*, June 8, 2018. https://news.artnet.com/exhibitions/oprah-winfrey-smithsonian-museum-show-1299806

Dwyer, Colin. "USPS Picks Perfect Line for Maya Angelou Stamp—If Only It Were Hers." NPR, April 8, 2015. https://www.npr.org/sections/thetwo-way/2015/04/08/398317105/maya-angelous-forever-stamp-forever-in-error

Forbes, Moira. "Oprah Winfrey Talks Philanthropy, Failure and What Every Guest—Including Beyonce—Asks Her." *Forbes*, September 18, 2012. https://www.forbes.com/sites/moiraforbes/2012/09/18/oprah-winfrey-talks-philanthropy-failure-and-what-every-guest-including-beyonce-asks-her/?sh=69aabd176bc0

Killoran, Ellen. "For Oprah Winfrey, Maya Angelou's Death Especially Personal." *International Business Times*, May 28, 2014. https://www.ibtimes.com/oprah-winfrey-maya-angelous-death-especially-personal-1591519

Krznarik, Roman. *Carpe Diem Regained*. New York: Penguin Random House, 2017.

Martin, Roland. "Roland Martin Interviews Oprah about Her Relationship with Maya Angelou." YouTube, April 12, 2014.

Miller, Mike. "Oprah Winfrey on How Her 'Mother Figure' Maya Angelou Inspired Her *A Wrinkle in Time* Character." *People*, May 29, 2018. https://people.com/movies/oprah-winfrey-maya-angelou-inspired-wrinkle-time-character/

Oldenburg, Ann. "Oprah Remembers Maya Angelou as 'Mentor, Mother/Sister, and Friend.'" *USA Today*, May 28, 2014. https://www.usatoday.com/story/life/entertainthis/2014/05/28/oprah-remembers-maya-angelou-as-mentor-mothersister-and-friend/77454026/

"Oprah Winfrey Mourns Maya Angelou." UPI. *U.S. News*, May 29, 2014. https://www.upi.com/Top_News/US/2014/05/29/Oprah-Winfrey-mourns-Maya-Angelou/7561401405406/

Oprah.com "How Dr. Maya Angelou Became San Francisco's First Black Streetcar Conductor." *Super Soul Sunday*, Season 4, Episode 410, May 12, 2013. http://www.oprah.com/own-super-soul-sunday/maya-angelou-san-franciscos-first-black-streetcar-conductor-video

Salley, Columbus. *The Black 100: A Ranking of the Most Influential African-Americans, Past and Present* (New York: Citadel Press1999).

Thompson, Krissah. "Honored by National Portrait Gallery, Maya Angelou Faces Mortality and Immortality." *The Washington Post*. April 6, 2014. https://www.washingtonpost.com/lifestyle/style/honored-by-national-portrait-gallery-maya-angelou-faces-mortality-and-immortality/2014/04/06/fa650922-bd27-11e3-bcec-b71ee10e9bc3_story.html

Walk-Morris, Tatiana. "Oprah and the Clintons Celebrate Maya Angelou in a New Documentary." *Vice*, February 21, 2017. https://www.vice.com/en_us/article/vvxbx9/oprah-and-the-clintons-celebrate-maya-angelou-in-a-new-documentary

WEB Staff, "Oprah Posts Loving Tribute to Maya Angelou." CBS Channel 6, Mary 28, 2014. https://wtvr.com/2014/05/28/oprah-tribute-to-maya-angelou/

Winfrey, Oprah. "Oprah Talks to Maya Angelou." *O, the Oprah Magazine*, December 2000. http://www.oprah.com/omagazine/oprah-interviews-maya-angelou

Winfrey, Oprah. "Oprah Winfrey's Golden Globes Cecil B. DeMille Speech—In Full." *The Telegraph*, January 8, 2018. https://www.telegraph.co.uk/films/2018/01/08/oprah-winfreys-golden-globes-cecil-b-demille-speech-full/

Winfrey, Oprah. "The Most Fun I Ever Had." *O, the Oprah Magazine*, May 2002. http://www.oprah.com/omagazine/the-most-fun-i-ever-had

Glossary

activist (AK-tih-vist)—A person who works toward a political or social goal.

assassinate (uh-SASS-ih-nayt)—To murder, usually for political reasons.

celestial (suh-LES-tee-ul)—Having to do with the stars or the sky.

inauguration (in-aw-gyur-AY-shun)—The act of placing somebody in an official position, as with a president.

mentor (MEN-tor)—An experienced adviser, teacher, or trainer.

mutism (MYOO-tism)—The inability to speak.

persevere (per-seh-VEER)—To endure or keep going, even in the face of tough odds.

philanthropist (fih-LAN-throh-pist)—A person who gives money to worthy causes.

pretension (pree-TEN-shun)—Behavior that is fake; the illusion of having greater importance or status than one does.

supernova (SOO-per-noh-vah)—A star that explodes with great intensity; a superstar.

trajectory (trah-JEK-tur-ee)—The path of an object moving through space; the path one chooses for a career.

validate (VAL-ih-dayt)—To confirm the truth of something.